DATE :

What whisper pulled me away from Allah today, and how did I respond?

Did I make an excuse to avoid doing what's right? Where do I think that came from?

If that same test came tomorrow, how would I respond differently for Allah's sake?

Was there a moment I chose Allah over my desires, even if no one saw it?

What do I want to ask Allah tonight, in regret, in hope, or in longing?

This section is for you to write whatever's in your heart

DATE :

What whisper pulled me away from Allah today, and how did I respond?

Did I make an excuse to avoid doing what's right? Where do I think that came from?

If that same test came tomorrow, how would I respond differently for Allah's sake?

Was there a moment I chose Allah over my desires, even if no one saw it?

What do I want to ask Allah tonight, in regret, in hope, or in longing?

This section is for you to write whatever's in your heart

DATE :

What whisper pulled me away from Allah today, and how did I respond?

Did I make an excuse to avoid doing what's right? Where do I think that came from?

If that same test came tomorrow, how would I respond differently for Allah's sake?

Was there a moment I chose Allah over my desires, even if no one saw it?

What do I want to ask Allah tonight, in regret, in hope, or in longing?

This section is for you to write whatever's in your heart

DATE :

What whisper pulled me away from Allah today, and how did I respond?

Did I make an excuse to avoid doing what's right? Where do I think that came from?

If that same test came tomorrow, how would I respond differently for Allah's sake?

Was there a moment I chose Allah over my desires, even if no one saw it?

What do I want to ask Allah tonight, in regret, in hope, or in longing?

This section is for you to write whatever's in your heart

DATE :

What whisper pulled me away from Allah today, and how did I respond?

Did I make an excuse to avoid doing what's right? Where do I think that came from?

If that same test came tomorrow, how would I respond differently for Allah's sake?

Was there a moment I chose Allah over my desires, even if no one saw it?

What do I want to ask Allah tonight, in regret, in hope, or in longing?

This section is for you to write whatever's in your heart

DATE :

What whisper pulled me away from Allah today, and how did I respond?

Did I make an excuse to avoid doing what's right? Where do I think that came from?

If that same test came tomorrow, how would I respond differently for Allah's sake?

Was there a moment I chose Allah over my desires, even if no one saw it?

What do I want to ask Allah tonight, in regret, in hope, or in longing?

This section is for you to write whatever's in your heart

DATE :

What whisper pulled me away from Allah today, and how did I respond?

Did I make an excuse to avoid doing what's right? Where do I think that came from?

If that same test came tomorrow, how would I respond differently for Allah's sake?

Was there a moment I chose Allah over my desires, even if no one saw it?

What do I want to ask Allah tonight, in regret, in hope, or in longing?

This section is for you to write whatever's in your heart

DATE :

What whisper pulled me away from Allah today, and how did I respond?

Did I make an excuse to avoid doing what's right? Where do I think that came from?

If that same test came tomorrow, how would I respond differently for Allah's sake?

Was there a moment I chose Allah over my desires, even if no one saw it?

What do I want to ask Allah tonight, in regret, in hope, or in longing?

This section is for you to write whatever's in your heart

DATE :

What whisper pulled me away from Allah today, and how did I respond?

Did I make an excuse to avoid doing what's right? Where do I think that came from?

If that same test came tomorrow, how would I respond differently for Allah's sake?

Was there a moment I chose Allah over my desires, even if no one saw it?

What do I want to ask Allah tonight, in regret, in hope, or in longing?

This section is for you to write whatever's in your heart

DATE :

What whisper pulled me away from Allah today, and how did I respond?

Did I make an excuse to avoid doing what's right? Where do I think that came from?

If that same test came tomorrow, how would I respond differently for Allah's sake?

Was there a moment I chose Allah over my desires, even if no one saw it?

What do I want to ask Allah tonight, in regret, in hope, or in longing?

This section is for you to write whatever's in your heart

DATE :

What whisper pulled me away from Allah today, and how did I respond?

Did I make an excuse to avoid doing what's right? Where do I think that came from?

If that same test came tomorrow, how would I respond differently for Allah's sake?

Was there a moment I chose Allah over my desires, even if no one saw it?

What do I want to ask Allah tonight, in regret, in hope, or in longing?

This section is for you to write whatever's in your heart

DATE :

What whisper pulled me away from Allah today, and how did I respond?

Did I make an excuse to avoid doing what's right? Where do I think that came from?

If that same test came tomorrow, how would I respond differently for Allah's sake?

Was there a moment I chose Allah over my desires, even if no one saw it?

What do I want to ask Allah tonight, in regret, in hope, or in longing?

This section is for you to write whatever's in your heart

DATE :

What whisper pulled me away from Allah today, and how did I respond?

Did I make an excuse to avoid doing what's right? Where do I think that came from?

If that same test came tomorrow, how would I respond differently for Allah's sake?

Was there a moment I chose Allah over my desires, even if no one saw it?

What do I want to ask Allah tonight, in regret, in hope, or in longing?

This section is for you to write whatever's in your heart

DATE :

What whisper pulled me away from Allah today, and how did I respond?

Did I make an excuse to avoid doing what's right? Where do I think that came from?

If that same test came tomorrow, how would I respond differently for Allah's sake?

Was there a moment I chose Allah over my desires, even if no one saw it?

What do I want to ask Allah tonight, in regret, in hope, or in longing?

This section is for you to write whatever's in your heart

DATE :

What whisper pulled me away from Allah today, and how did I respond?

Did I make an excuse to avoid doing what's right? Where do I think that came from?

If that same test came tomorrow, how would I respond differently for Allah's sake?

Was there a moment I chose Allah over my desires, even if no one saw it?

What do I want to ask Allah tonight, in regret, in hope, or in longing?

This section is for you to write whatever's in your heart

DATE :

What whisper pulled me away from Allah today, and how did I respond?

Did I make an excuse to avoid doing what's right? Where do I think that came from?

If that same test came tomorrow, how would I respond differently for Allah's sake?

Was there a moment I chose Allah over my desires, even if no one saw it?

What do I want to ask Allah tonight, in regret, in hope, or in longing?

This section is for you to write whatever's in your heart

DATE :

What whisper pulled me away from Allah today, and how did I respond?

Did I make an excuse to avoid doing what's right? Where do I think that came from?

If that same test came tomorrow, how would I respond differently for Allah's sake?

Was there a moment I chose Allah over my desires, even if no one saw it?

What do I want to ask Allah tonight, in regret, in hope, or in longing?

This section is for you to write whatever's in your heart

DATE :

What whisper pulled me away from Allah today, and how did I respond?

Did I make an excuse to avoid doing what's right? Where do I think that came from?

If that same test came tomorrow, how would I respond differently for Allah's sake?

Was there a moment I chose Allah over my desires, even if no one saw it?

What do I want to ask Allah tonight, in regret, in hope, or in longing?

This section is for you to write whatever's in your heart

DATE :

What whisper pulled me away from Allah today, and how did I respond?

Did I make an excuse to avoid doing what's right? Where do I think that came from?

If that same test came tomorrow, how would I respond differently for Allah's sake?

Was there a moment I chose Allah over my desires, even if no one saw it?

What do I want to ask Allah tonight, in regret, in hope, or in longing?

This section is for you to write whatever's in your heart

DATE :

What whisper pulled me away from Allah today, and how did I respond?

Did I make an excuse to avoid doing what's right? Where do I think that came from?

If that same test came tomorrow, how would I respond differently for Allah's sake?

Was there a moment I chose Allah over my desires, even if no one saw it?

What do I want to ask Allah tonight, in regret, in hope, or in longing?

This section is for you to write whatever's in your heart

DATE :

What whisper pulled me away from Allah today, and how did I respond?

Did I make an excuse to avoid doing what's right? Where do I think that came from?

If that same test came tomorrow, how would I respond differently for Allah's sake?

Was there a moment I chose Allah over my desires, even if no one saw it?

What do I want to ask Allah tonight, in regret, in hope, or in longing?

This section is for you to write whatever's in your heart

DATE :

What whisper pulled me away from Allah today, and how did I respond?

Did I make an excuse to avoid doing what's right? Where do I think that came from?

If that same test came tomorrow, how would I respond differently for Allah's sake?

Was there a moment I chose Allah over my desires, even if no one saw it?

What do I want to ask Allah tonight, in regret, in hope, or in longing?

This section is for you to write whatever's in your heart

DATE :

What whisper pulled me away from Allah today, and how did I respond?

Did I make an excuse to avoid doing what's right? Where do I think that came from?

If that same test came tomorrow, how would I respond differently for Allah's sake?

Was there a moment I chose Allah over my desires, even if no one saw it?

What do I want to ask Allah tonight, in regret, in hope, or in longing?

This section is for you to write whatever's in your heart

DATE :

What whisper pulled me away from Allah today, and how did I respond?

Did I make an excuse to avoid doing what's right? Where do I think that came from?

If that same test came tomorrow, how would I respond differently for Allah's sake?

Was there a moment I chose Allah over my desires, even if no one saw it?

What do I want to ask Allah tonight, in regret, in hope, or in longing?

This section is for you to write whatever's in your heart

DATE :

What whisper pulled me away from Allah today, and how did I respond?

Did I make an excuse to avoid doing what's right? Where do I think that came from?

If that same test came tomorrow, how would I respond differently for Allah's sake?

Was there a moment I chose Allah over my desires, even if no one saw it?

What do I want to ask Allah tonight, in regret, in hope, or in longing?

This section is for you to write whatever's in your heart

DATE :

What whisper pulled me away from Allah today, and how did I respond?

Did I make an excuse to avoid doing what's right? Where do I think that came from?

If that same test came tomorrow, how would I respond differently for Allah's sake?

Was there a moment I chose Allah over my desires, even if no one saw it?

What do I want to ask Allah tonight, in regret, in hope, or in longing?

This section is for you to write whatever's in your heart

DATE :

What whisper pulled me away from Allah today, and how did I respond?

Did I make an excuse to avoid doing what's right? Where do I think that came from?

If that same test came tomorrow, how would I respond differently for Allah's sake?

Was there a moment I chose Allah over my desires, even if no one saw it?

What do I want to ask Allah tonight, in regret, in hope, or in longing?

This section is for you to write whatever's in your heart

DATE :

What whisper pulled me away from Allah today, and how did I respond?

Did I make an excuse to avoid doing what's right? Where do I think that came from?

If that same test came tomorrow, how would I respond differently for Allah's sake?

Was there a moment I chose Allah over my desires, even if no one saw it?

What do I want to ask Allah tonight, in regret, in hope, or in longing?

This section is for you to write whatever's in your heart

DATE :

What whisper pulled me away from Allah today, and how did I respond?

Did I make an excuse to avoid doing what's right? Where do I think that came from?

If that same test came tomorrow, how would I respond differently for Allah's sake?

Was there a moment I chose Allah over my desires, even if no one saw it?

What do I want to ask Allah tonight, in regret, in hope, or in longing?

This section is for you to write whatever's in your heart

DATE :

What whisper pulled me away from Allah today, and how did I respond?

Did I make an excuse to avoid doing what's right? Where do I think that came from?

If that same test came tomorrow, how would I respond differently for Allah's sake?

Was there a moment I chose Allah over my desires, even if no one saw it?

What do I want to ask Allah tonight, in regret, in hope, or in longing?

This section is for you to write whatever's in your heart

DATE :

What whisper pulled me away from Allah today, and how did I respond?

Did I make an excuse to avoid doing what's right? Where do I think that came from?

If that same test came tomorrow, how would I respond differently for Allah's sake?

Was there a moment I chose Allah over my desires, even if no one saw it?

What do I want to ask Allah tonight, in regret, in hope, or in longing?

This section is for you to write whatever's in your heart

DATE :

What whisper pulled me away from Allah today, and how did I respond?

Did I make an excuse to avoid doing what's right? Where do I think that came from?

If that same test came tomorrow, how would I respond differently for Allah's sake?

Was there a moment I chose Allah over my desires, even if no one saw it?

What do I want to ask Allah tonight, in regret, in hope, or in longing?

This section is for you to write whatever's in your heart

DATE :

What whisper pulled me away from Allah today, and how did I respond?

Did I make an excuse to avoid doing what's right? Where do I think that came from?

If that same test came tomorrow, how would I respond differently for Allah's sake?

Was there a moment I chose Allah over my desires, even if no one saw it?

What do I want to ask Allah tonight, in regret, in hope, or in longing?

This section is for you to write whatever's in your heart

DATE :

What whisper pulled me away from Allah today, and how did I respond?

Did I make an excuse to avoid doing what's right? Where do I think that came from?

If that same test came tomorrow, how would I respond differently for Allah's sake?

Was there a moment I chose Allah over my desires, even if no one saw it?

What do I want to ask Allah tonight, in regret, in hope, or in longing?

This section is for you to write whatever's in your heart

DATE :

What whisper pulled me away from Allah today, and how did I respond?

Did I make an excuse to avoid doing what's right? Where do I think that came from?

If that same test came tomorrow, how would I respond differently for Allah's sake?

Was there a moment I chose Allah over my desires, even if no one saw it?

What do I want to ask Allah tonight, in regret, in hope, or in longing?

This section is for you to write whatever's in your heart

DATE :

What whisper pulled me away from Allah today, and how did I respond?

Did I make an excuse to avoid doing what's right? Where do I think that came from?

If that same test came tomorrow, how would I respond differently for Allah's sake?

Was there a moment I chose Allah over my desires, even if no one saw it?

What do I want to ask Allah tonight, in regret, in hope, or in longing?

This section is for you to write whatever's in your heart

DATE :

What whisper pulled me away from Allah today, and how did I respond?

Did I make an excuse to avoid doing what's right? Where do I think that came from?

If that same test came tomorrow, how would I respond differently for Allah's sake?

Was there a moment I chose Allah over my desires, even if no one saw it?

What do I want to ask Allah tonight, in regret, in hope, or in longing?

This section is for you to write whatever's in your heart

DATE :

What whisper pulled me away from Allah today, and how did I respond?

Did I make an excuse to avoid doing what's right? Where do I think that came from?

If that same test came tomorrow, how would I respond differently for Allah's sake?

Was there a moment I chose Allah over my desires, even if no one saw it?

What do I want to ask Allah tonight, in regret, in hope, or in longing?

This section is for you to write whatever's in your heart

DATE :

What whisper pulled me away from Allah today, and how did I respond?

Did I make an excuse to avoid doing what's right? Where do I think that came from?

If that same test came tomorrow, how would I respond differently for Allah's sake?

Was there a moment I chose Allah over my desires, even if no one saw it?

What do I want to ask Allah tonight, in regret, in hope, or in longing?

This section is for you to write whatever's in your heart

DATE :

What whisper pulled me away from Allah today, and how did I respond?

Did I make an excuse to avoid doing what's right? Where do I think that came from?

If that same test came tomorrow, how would I respond differently for Allah's sake?

Was there a moment I chose Allah over my desires, even if no one saw it?

What do I want to ask Allah tonight, in regret, in hope, or in longing?

This section is for you to write whatever's in your heart